WIND INSTRUMENTS

by ANITA GANERI

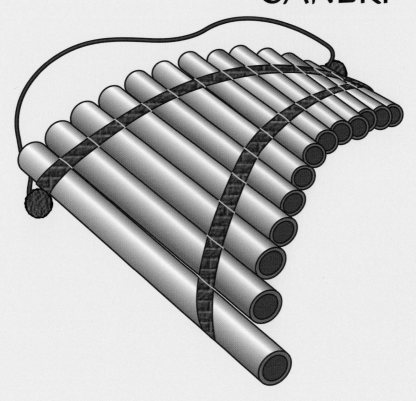

A+

Smart Apple Media

Published by Smart Apple Media
P.O. Box 3263, Mankato, Minnesota 56002

Printed in the United States of America at Corporate Graphics, in North Mankato, Minnesota.

Library of Congress Cataloging-in-Publication Data
Ganeri, Anita, 1961-
  Wind instruments / by Anita Ganeri.
      p. cm. -- (How the world makes music)
  Includes index.
  Summary: "Describes various wind instruments from around the world, such as the familiar
clarinet, saxophone, and flute, along with other traditional instruments such as the Chinese flute,
nose flute, and pan pipes"--Provided by publisher.
  ISBN 978-1-59920-482-6 (library binding)
  1. Wind instruments--Juvenile literature. I. Title.
  ML930.G36 2012
  788'.19--dc22

                          2010042423

Created by Appleseed Editions, Ltd.
Designed by Guy Callaby
Illustrated by Graham Rosewarne
Edited by Jinny Johnson
Picture research by Su Alexander

Picture credits:
l = left, r = right, t = top, b = bottom
Title page left to right Photo Japan/Alamy, Lebrecht Music & Arts Picture Library/Alamy, Svemir/Shutterstock, Edwin
Remsberg/Alamy; Contents page John James/Alamy; Page 4 Sergey Lavrentev/Shutterstock; 5t Lebrecht Music & Arts
Picture Library/Alamy, b Photofusion/Alamy; 6 Jules Studio/Shutterstock; 7 Lebrecht Music & Arts; 8 Photo Japan/Alamy;
9 Nagib/Shutterstock; 10 David Hancock/Alamy; 11 Edwin Remsberg/Alamy; 12 Lawrence Wee/Shutterstock; 13t Alex
Ramsay/Alamy, b Terry Harris Just Greece Photo Library/Alamy; 14 Svemir/Shutterstock; 15 Lebrecht Music & Arts Picture
Library/Alamy; 16 Keith Morris/Alamy; 17t Craig Lovell/Eagle Visions Photography/Alamy, b Robert Fried/Alamy; 19t
Oksana.Perkins/Shutterstock, b Lebrecht Music & Arts Picture Library/Alamy; 21t Arterra Picture library/Alamy, b John
James/Alamy; 22 The Art Gallery Collection/Alamy; 23 Lebrecht Music & Arts Picture Library/Alamy; 24 Anna
Chelnokova/Shutterstock; 25 Lebrecht Music & Arts Picture Library/Alamy; 26 Lebrecht Music & Arts; 27t Robert Harding
Picture Library/Alamy, b Lebrecht Music & Arts Picture Library/Alamy; 29 Nathan Benn/Alamy.
Front cover: Main pic of Chinese flute player, Chen Heng Kong/Shutterstock; Grayscale b/g image of keys, Heidi Hart/
Shutterstock; Snake charmer, Oksana.Perkins/Shutterstock; Oboist, Anna Chelnokova/Shutterstock; Flautist, Svemir/
Shutterstock; Pan pipes player, Lawrence Wee/Shutterstock

DAD0047
3-2011

9 8 7 6 5 4 3 2 1

Contents

Wind Instruments

People make music all around the world. They play musical instruments and sing songs when they are happy or sad. Music is often part of festivals and other ceremonies. For most people, listening to music is important in their everyday lives.

Musical Pipes

There are many different types of musical instruments. This book is about wind instruments. Most wind instruments are basically hollow tubes. The player usually blows into the end of the tube, called the mouthpiece. As the air travels down the tube, it vibrates. This vibrating air makes the sound that you hear.

The clarinet is a wind instrument. The player blows into the mouthpiece and the air travels down the tube.

Musical Notes

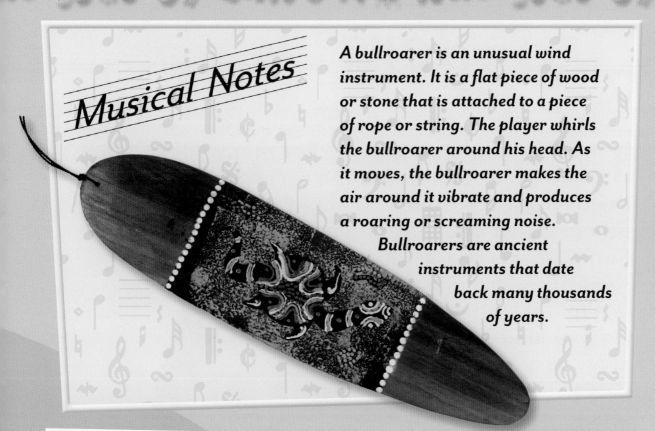

A bullroarer is an unusual wind instrument. It is a flat piece of wood or stone that is attached to a piece of rope or string. The player whirls the bullroarer around his head. As it moves, the bullroarer makes the air around it vibrate and produces a roaring or screaming noise. Bullroarers are ancient instruments that date back many thousands of years.

Students play a variety of wind instruments during a school music lesson.

Recorders

The first wind instrument that many people learn to play is the recorder. The descant recorder you might play at school is just one of a whole family of recorders. The little sopranino is about 9 inches (23 cm) long and plays very high notes. The treble, tenor, and bass recorders are all longer than the descant. They make deeper sounds.

The recorder has holes that are covered and uncovered by the player's fingers. This changes the pitch of the note being played.

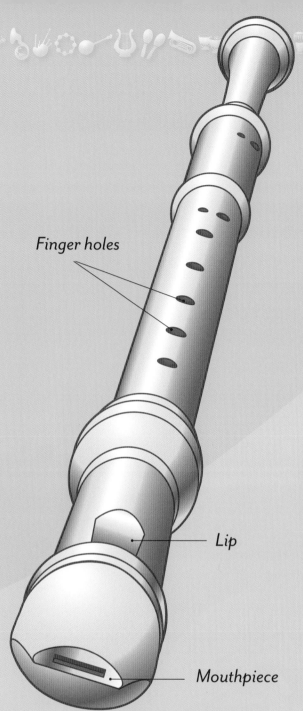

Finger holes

Lip

Mouthpiece

Playing the Recorder

To play the recorder, you put the mouthpiece into your mouth and blow gently into it. The air travels down a thin channel in the mouthpiece until it hits the sharp edge of the lip below. This movement makes the air inside the recorder vibrate.

Musical Notes

Today, recorders are usually made from wood or plastic. In the past, some recorders were carved from ivory. Others were beautifully decorated with carved patterns. This angel plays a recorder in a painting by Giovanni Bellini, an Italian Renaissance artist.

Shakuhachi

Mouthpiece

The shakuhachi is a Japanese flute. It is made from bamboo. The player holds the instrument downward and blows across the hole at the top, like blowing across the top of a bottle. The shakuhachi is an ancient instrument that was played by Buddhist monks. It is still very popular in Japan, and it is often heard in pop and jazz music.

Finger holes

Musical Notes

In the past, when Buddhist monks played their shakuhachis, they often wore wicker baskets over their heads. The monks wore the baskets to show that they were separate from the world and people around them.

Chinese Flute

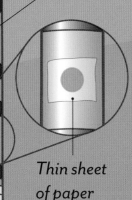

Mouth hole

Thin sheet of paper

Finger holes

T he Chinese flute is usually made from bamboo and known as a dizi. The player holds it sideways and blows across the mouth hole to make a sound. The dizi has a hole that is covered by a thin sheet of paper. When the air vibrates inside the flute, the paper also vibrates, making a buzzing sound.

Musical Notes

Some of these flutes have a dragon head at one end and its tail at the other. In the past, these beautiful dragon flutes were played at religious ceremonies.

Nose Flutes

Did you know that you can play a flute with your nose? In some parts of the world, flutes that are played by breathing through a nostril are very popular. There are many different kinds of nose flutes played all over the Pacific region and in Africa.

Nguru

In New Zealand, the Maori people play a nose flute called a nguru. It is usually carved from wood or stone and beautifully decorated. The player breathes gently into a hole on the top to make a sound.

This Maori nose flute is carved out of wood. The gentle sound of the nose flute is often used to mark times of birth or death.

Bamboo Breath

Many nose flutes are made from a piece of hollow bamboo. The player closes one nostril with one hand and holds the flute with the other hand. The sound of the nose flute is very gentle and sweet.

A man plays a nose flute, closing one nostril with his right hand.

Breath hole

Bamboo Flute

Musical Notes

In Polynesia, many people believe that breath from the nose is purer than breath from the mouth. This makes the music of the nose flute very special. In the past, men used to play the nose flute to woo their sweethearts.

Panpipes

The panpipes are made from a row of tubes of different lengths, all joined together. The tubes are closed at one end. The player blows across the open end to play a note. Every pipe plays a different note, depending on its length. The short pipes play higher notes. The longer the pipe, the deeper the note.

Panpipes make a gentle, airy sound, which is very popular.

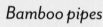

Bamboo pipes

Pipes held together with strips of material

Ancient Instrument

The panpipes are thousands of years old and are played all over the world. They are made from many different materials, including bamboo, clay, and stone.

Musical Notes

An ancient Greek myth tells the story of the god Pan, who fell in love with Syrinx, a water nymph. Syrinx ran away and changed into a reed to escape him. Pan cut the reed and joined its pieces together to make the first set of panpipes.

Zampona

In the Andes Mountains of Peru, panpipes are called zampona. They come in many different sizes, and are often played by large groups of musicians.

Musicians in Peru, South America, play the zampona. The longest pipes have the deepest sounds.

Flute

The flute that is played in a concert band or orchestra is usually made from metal. The player holds it sideways and blows across an oval-shaped hole in the mouthpiece.

A flute player, or flutist, holds the instrument sideways to play it.

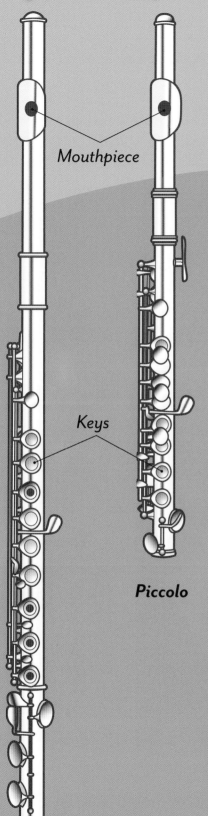

Mouthpiece

Keys

Piccolo

Flute

Musical Notes

The flute has a much shorter relative called the piccolo. The piccolo is about 12.5 inches (32 cm) long and plays very high notes— the highest in the whole band or orchestra.

Changing the Note

The metal body of the flute has holes that can be covered and uncovered. To block the holes, the player presses down keys that have soft pads underneath. If all the holes in the flute are blocked, the air vibrates down the whole length of the tube. This produces a deep note. If the player uncovers some of the holes, the length of the vibrating air is shorter. This produces a higher note. This is how players make different notes on a wind instrument.

Clarinet

The clarinet has a thin strip of cane, called a reed, attached to its mouthpiece. When the player blows into the mouthpiece, the reed vibrates. The reed gives the clarinet its own very recognizable sound.

Origins

The clarinet was invented in about 1700 by a German instrument-maker named Johann Christoph Denner. He took an older instrument called a chalumeau and updated it.

Mouthpiece

Keys and finger holes

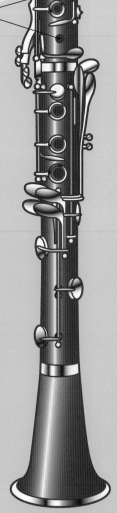

A girl practices playing her clarinet.

Sound Effects

The clarinet is usually made from wood and has metal keys. The player holds the instrument downward. The clarinet has a very adaptable sound and can play some spectacular sound effects. It is very popular in jazz music.

Don Byron, a New York jazz clarinetist, plays at the Monterey Jazz Festival in California.

Musical Notes

The clarinet is very popular in Greece. It is often played at weddings and in dance music. It is also an important instrument in Jewish klezmer music.

Double Clarinet

Sometimes two wind instruments are fastened together and are both blown at the same time by one player. Double clarinets are very popular in the Middle East and India.

This double clarinet is made from two bamboo pipes that have been tied together. Both of the pipes have holes to play melodies.

Two Pipes

In Egypt, the double clarinet is called an arghul. In Iraq, it is a zummara. Sometimes, both pipes have holes that the player can cover and uncover to sound different notes. Other double clarinets have one pipe with holes and one drone pipe. The drone pipe has no holes, so when it is blown, it always plays the same note.

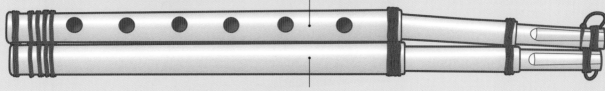

Melody pipe

Drone pipe

Musical Notes

In India, there is a type of double clarinet called the tiktiri. It has two pipes stuck into the dried-out shell of a gourd. The player blows into the gourd and down the pipes. The tiktiri was traditionally used by snake charmers.

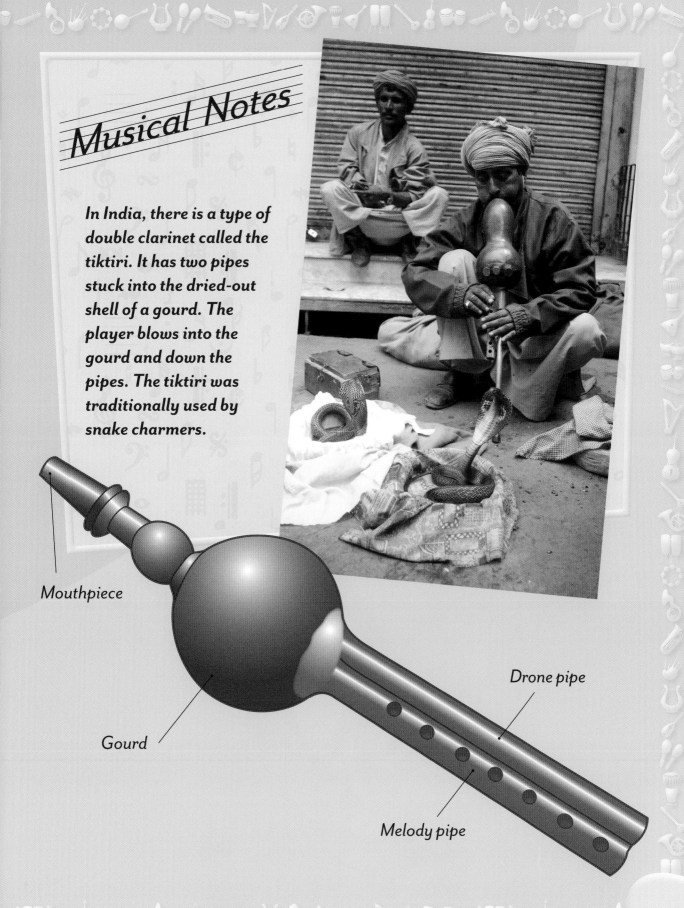

Mouthpiece

Gourd

Drone pipe

Melody pipe

Saxophone

The saxophone is a metal wind instrument. Like the clarinet, it has a single reed in its mouthpiece. The saxophone was invented in the 1840s by a Belgian instrument maker named Adolphe Sax. He attached the mouthpiece of a clarinet to the body and keys of an oboe. Sax designed his new instrument to be played in military bands. But in the 20th century, it also became a very popular instrument in jazz and pop music.

Mouthpiece with reed

Neck

Keys

Ring for strap

Bell

The "Sax" Family

Adolphe Sax originally made saxophones in 14 different sizes. Today, only four of these are widely played—the soprano, alto, tenor, and baritone.

This statue of Adolphe Sax is in front of his birthplace at Dinant, Belgium.

Musical Notes

There have been many famous saxophone players in the world of jazz, including Charlie Parker and John Coltrane. Here, British jazz saxophonist Soweto Kinch plays at a concert in the U.K.

Shawm

During the Renaissance period (about 1400 to 1600), shawms were widely played in Europe. A shawm was a double reed instrument. This meant that it had a mouthpiece made from two pieces of cane, stuck firmly together. When a player blew through the double reed, the two pieces of cane vibrated. The vibrations traveled down the air in the instrument to produce a piercing sound.

Noisy Shawms

Shawms were very loud instruments. For this reason, they were usually played outdoors. Shawms were sometimes played in military bands to frighten the enemy. They were also used to play dance music.

Angels play shawms (left) and a trombone (right) in a painting by a Renaissance artist.

A man plays a shawm in Goa, India.

Double reed

Wooden body

Finger holes

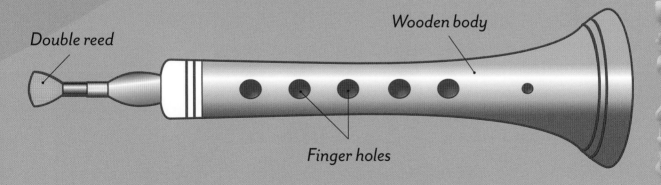

Musical Notes

The great-bass shawm was 9 feet (2.7 meters) long. To play this massive instrument, the musician had to stand on a stool to reach the mouthpiece.

Oboe

The oboe developed from the Renaissance shawm. It was the result of lots of experiments to make a quieter type of shawm that could be played indoors. The name oboe comes from the French *hautbois* meaning "high wood." The earliest oboes were played at the court of the French king, Louis XIV, in the mid-1600s.

Woodwind Section

Today, the oboe is part of the woodwind section of a Western orchestra. Other woodwind instruments are the flute, clarinet, and bassoon. The oboe has a piercing and often sad sound.

Double reed mouthpiece fits into the top of the instrument   *Keys*

Bassoon

The bassoon plays the lowest notes in the woodwind section of the orchestra. It has a double reed like the oboe. The reed is attached to the end of a piece of curved metal tubing, called the crook. The bassoon is quite big and heavy, so the player either rests it on the floor, or hangs it off a neck sling.

Double reed

Crook

Keys

Musical Notes

The bassoon has an even bigger relative. The contra-bassoon (or double bassoon) has a gentle, deep sound. It plays notes an octave (eight notes) below the bassoon.

This player is using a neck sling to support the bassoon's weight.

Ancient Reeds

Instruments with double reeds have been played since ancient times. Pictures on ancient Greek vases and carvings show people playing an instrument made of two thin pipes. The pipes are connected to a double reed that is blown by the player. This instrument was called an aulos.

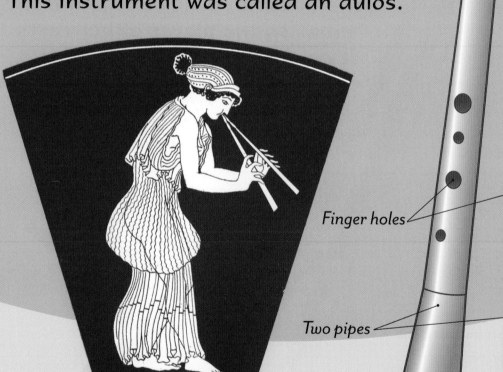

Finger holes

Two pipes

This picture, in the style of an ancient Greek vase painting, shows a woman with an aulos.

Aulos Sounds

The aulos was played at the theater and at religious ceremonies. It was also used to accompany sporting events and wrestling matches.

Shanai

In India, the shanai is a double reed instrument that is played mainly in the north of the country. It is played in processions and at marriages, and its sound is thought to bring good fortune. Sometimes, two shahnai are tied together to make a double instrument, rather like the aulos.

Ustad Bismillah Khan, a shahnai player and one of India's best-known musicians.

Musical Notes

In the south of India, the best-known double reed instrument is called the nagasvaram. It produces a loud noise from a slender pipe that can be more than 2.5 feet (80 cm) long.

Bagpipes

The sound of the bagpipes is most often heard in Scotland and in Scottish music. But different types of bagpipes are played across Asia, North Africa, and Europe.

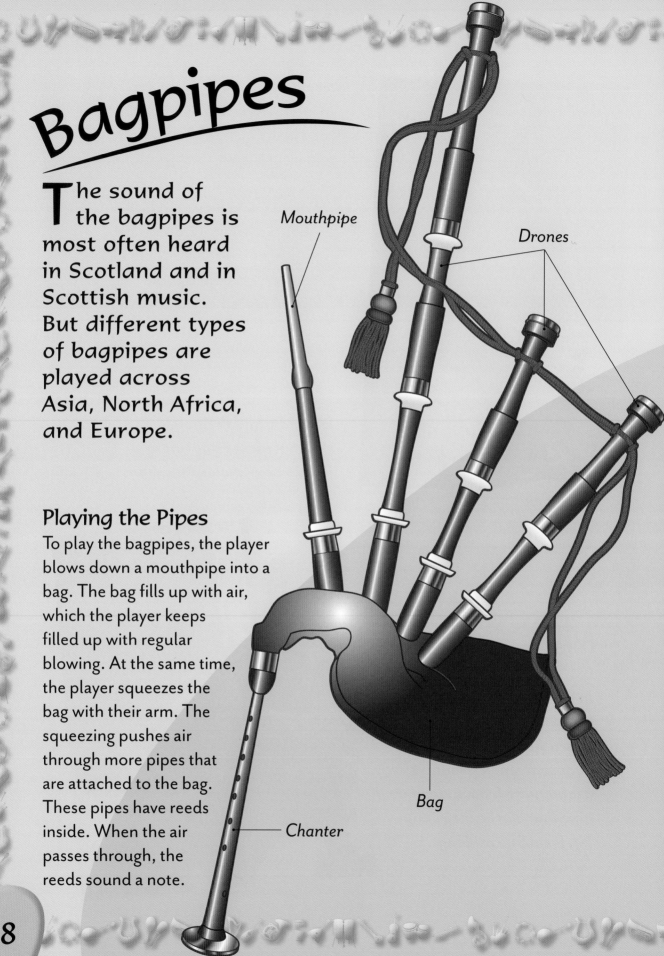

Mouthpipe

Drones

Bag

Playing the Pipes

To play the bagpipes, the player blows down a mouthpipe into a bag. The bag fills up with air, which the player keeps filled up with regular blowing. At the same time, the player squeezes the bag with their arm. The squeezing pushes air through more pipes that are attached to the bag. These pipes have reeds inside. When the air passes through, the reeds sound a note.

Chanter

A marching band of bagpipers performs during a soccer game in Glasgow, Scotland.

Chanter and Drone

One of the pipes attached to the bag has holes drilled into it. The bagpipe player covers and uncovers the holes to sound different notes. This pipe is called the chanter. Other pipes have no holes and are drone pipes.

Musical Notes

People have used all sorts of different materials to make bagpipe bags. Traditional bags are made of skins from animals, such as sheep, goats, pigs, or cows. Some modern bags are made from rubber and even Gore-Tex (the material used to make waterproof jackets and shoes).

Words to Remember

bamboo
a type of woody grass that has a hollow stem

bass
a low-pitched sound

Buddhist
a follower of Buddhism, a religion based on the teachings of Siddhartha Gautama, the Buddha

crook
the curved piece of metal tubing that holds the mouthpiece of a bassoon

double reed
a mouthpiece made from two pieces of cane that are stuck together

drone
an accompaniment that remains at the same pitch, or group of pitches, throughout a piece of music

gourd
a type of fruit with a thick skin; gourds can be hollowed out and dried to make musical instruments.

ivory
a hard, yellowish-white material that elephant tusks are made of; the use of ivory is no longer allowed.

key
a lever on an instrument that is used to cover and uncover a hole

klezmer
a type of Jewish folk music that originally came from Eastern Europe

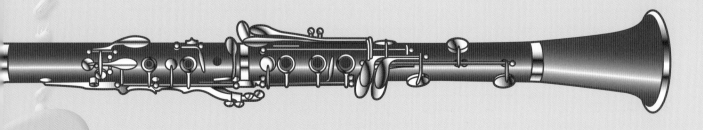

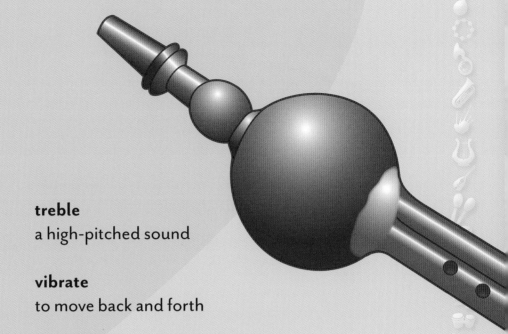

mouthpiece
the part of a wind instrument that is placed in the mouth to blow through

pitch
how high or low a musical note is

reed
a thin strip of shaped cane

treble
a high-pitched sound

vibrate
to move back and forth

woodwind
a group of muscial instruments that includes flutes, oboes, and clarinets; a wind instrument makes a sound when it is blown into.

The Recorder Family
From the highest pitch to the lowest pitch:
- sopranino
- descant (soprano)
- treble
- tenor
- bass
- great bass

The Saxophone Family
The most common saxophones, from the highest pitch to the lowest pitch:
- soprano
- alto
- tenor
- baritone

Web Sites

Medieval Life and Times: Woodwind Instruments
http://www.medieval-life-and-times.info/medieval-music/woodwind-instruments.htm

San Francisco Symphony Kids: Instruments of the Orchestra
http://www.sfskids.org/templates/instorchframe.asp?pageid=3

Sphinx Kids! Instrument Storage Room
http://www.sphinxkids.org/Instrument_Storage.html

Woodwind Instruments by Classics for Kids
http://www.classicsforkids.com/music/instruments_list.asp?family=Woodwind

Index